TIPS FOR #COLLEGE LIFE

POWERFUL COLLEGE ADVICE FOR EXCELLING AS A
COLLEGE FRESHMAN

BUKKY EKINE-OGUNLANA

COPYRIGHT

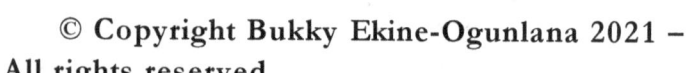

© **Copyright Bukky Ekine-Ogunlana 2021 – All rights reserved.**

The content contained within this book may not be reproduced, duplicated or transmitted without direct written permission from the author or the publisher.

Under no circumstance will any blame or legal responsibility be held against the publisher, or author, for any damages, reparation, or monetary loss due to the information contained within this book. Either directly or indirectly. You are responsible for your own choices, actions and results.

Legal Notice:

This book is copyright protected. This book is only for personal use. You cannot amend, distribute, sell, use, quote or paraphrase any part, or the content within this book, without the consent of the author or publisher.

Disclaimer Notice:

Please note the information contained within this document is for educational and entertainment purpose only. All effort has been executed to present accurate, up to date, and reliable, complete information. No warranties of any kind are declared or implied. Readers acknowledge that the author is not engaging in the rendering of legal, financial, medical or professional advice. The content within this book has been derived from various sources. Please consult a licensed professional before attempting any techniques outlined in this book

By reading this document, the reader agrees that under no circumstances is the author responsible for any losses, direct or indirect, which are incurred as a result of the use of the information contained within this document, including, but not limited to,—errors, omissions, or inaccuracies.

Published by

TCEC Publishing
TCEC House
14-18 Ada Street, London Fields,
E8 4QU, England, Great Britain.

TABLE OF CONTENTS

COPYRIGHT ii

INTRODUCTION vi

CHAPTER ONE STUDENTS LIFE IN THE COLLEGE 8

CHAPTER TWO HOW TO BE PREPARED AS A FRESHER 25

CHAPTER THREE IMPORTANT ORIENTATION OF A FRESHER 46

CHAPTER FOUR TIPS FOR INCOMING FRESHERS 53

CHAPTER FIVE HOW TO SURVIVE YOUR FRESHMAN YEAR 57

CHAPTER SIX HOW TO MAKE USE OF YOUR TIME IN THE COLLEGE 65

CHAPTER SEVEN EXCELLENT STUDENT 84

CHAPTER EIGHT COLLEGE ROOMMATE 92

CHAPTER NINE THREE KINGS 97

CHAPTER TEN OUTSTANDING STUDENT 107

CHAPTER ELEVEN HOW TO BE SAFE ON CAMPUS .. 113

CHAPTER TWELVE MONEY MANAGEMENT FOR STUDENTS 115

CHAPTER THIRTEEN COLLEGE HEALTH RISK 130

CHAPTER FOURTEEN STUDENTS CAMPUS FELLOWSHIP 133

CONCLUSION 137

INTRODUCTION

Leaving home for the first time and finally being independent. Well, not THAT independent as your parents are paying your way to college but independent in the sense that you would be living away from home for your college studies. That sounds better? Alright. Going to college for the first time is exciting – there's a lot of anticipation for all the new experiences and the first steps to becoming a grown up. So as a student, what do you do? How do you start your life? How do you act? Where would you live? What will you do?

The freedom that comes with leaving home for the first time will occupy most students' thoughts when it comes to the first year of college, but later on the reality of studying at the undergraduate level quickly dawn on many for whom the experience will quite often be a shock from the confines of the school classroom.

The first few weeks at university are amongst the busiest of a young adult's life, but the challenge of new learning styles and independent study can add to what is already a full plate of activities for most.

Put simply, college is very different from school regarding what is expected either in the lecture hall or the laboratory.

I would be incredibly thankful if you could take 60 seconds to write a brief review Amazon or the platform of purchase, even if it's just a few sentences!

CHAPTER ONE
STUDENTS LIFE IN THE COLLEGE

Waking up to the good news that I've made it to the college stirred up a mixed feeling in me. On the one hand, I was delighted that I would be gaining the freedom I've always longed for in some couple of weeks, after receiving the letter delivered by the postman. However, on the other hand, I became so worried and wondered what the new environment would look like.

Many questions flooded my heart. Will I still be woken up by my mother's scream for me to come down for my usual morning ritual of hot chocolate and sandwich? Will I sit with familiar faces that could provoke laughter out of your mouth the way Jesse and Becky do? Will I be able to handle the transformation I'm about to embrace? Will there be excitement that will propel catching of fun? Should I be looking forward to terrifying and jaw-breaking scenarios? These got me thinking really that for hours, answers didn't come to me.

TIPS FOR #COLLEGELIFE

Allow me to say this quickly if you're welcomed to the College of your Choice and ignorance filled your heart as regards what you need to know, where you need to go, whom you need to walk with, you may take the wrong foot which may affect your subsequent decision in the future.

Immediately my alarm went off around 6:00 am for the second time to alert me to get ready for my class, I rose up without giving it a second thought. I had no time to waste again and I hit the wall with my fist to make the light come back to life. Though a surprise look appeared boldly on my face seeing my roommates still fast asleep, I continued with my preparation feeling that they weren't in the same department with me. I headed straight to the shower. I began to think. *These people are freaking lazy, sleeping at this hour of the day?*

Upon my arrival on campus at around 7:00 am, I was greeted by mammoth of students going about their business. And since I'd not familiarised my face with any of them, I couldn't distinguish between students in their sophomore year and the junior or senior year. Even though I felt awkward walking towards my department with the help of the school's map with me, as soon as I walked past few of them, I took to my heels, and that generated raucous laughter amongst them.

A signpost read *THE ESTATE MANAGEMENT DEPARTMENT WELCOMES OUR FRESHMEN*. That I saw that alone gave me a relief that I've gotten to where I belonged. As I stepped into the alleyway in the department, my feet became so reluctant to carry me. I had to drop my head like a bag hung loosely on a tree. I staggered along and that caught the attention of those around. And I thought they were talking about me as every attempt to look gave me an eye's contact with some guy or lady wherever I faced.

With just two doors to the end of the hallway, on the lintel of the door was *ESTATE MANAGEMENT* boldly written. My heart melted away with enthusiasm that I'd finally escaped from their eyes glued on me. On entering the class, I saw no head in attendance. *Could I have entered the wrong class?* And as I was about exiting to see if the lecture was already going on elsewhere, I ran into an Indo-American stoutly built fat man on checkered tie and black suit. His moustache had tail, and his American

English was garnished with an Indian accent, which seemed quite funny.

Mocking him with his accent didn't last long as he flatly laughed at me after narrating my ordeal to him. Charles Samuel, the Management Professor, made a mess of me knowing that I never knew the class was slated for 9:00 am whereas I'd arrived two hours before the lecture. I felt pathetically embarrassed. Having discovered that how he handled the situation really hurt me, he apologised, tapped me on the back and went to his table.

How could I have cheaply made a fool of myself like that? Didn't I check the time well? It dawned on me that the anxiety that I was going to the College overwhelmed me that I didn't check the time.

The Management Professor rose to become one of the lecturers I loved dearly because he proved to me that he understood the nitty-gritty of the course. My outstanding feat in his class endeared me to him that he'd just joke about our first meeting each time he wanted to hand over my score sheets to me. At first, I frowned at that. But later, I became used to it.

Allow me to say this: the timing in the College is exceptionally different from that of the conventional secondary school timing. You're bound to experience a lot of flexibility with your classes at the College. Do not be in haste as to attending a class, else, you will feel embarrassed the way I felt on my first day on campus.

Perhaps, you were told to take a Math subject in your secondary school at maybe 10:00 am every day. In the College, you'll have to take Math courses with a lot of choices to be made. These courses will definitely be at different days, various times, and for diverse periods. With this alone, you know you're now in college.

Do you know that another good thing about College timing is the fact that you've got greater chances to survey your curiosities?

What you major in will determine the kind of classes you'll specialise in. Remember, when you were in secondary, you were given some curricular of classes that you will take across all subject areas. In the college as a freshman, begin to think of your timing like a pyramid.

As a sophomore, you'll definitely offer more general classes, which will give you ample opportunity to experience a mixture of many subjects that will make you garner knowledge all around, and a few classes in your major. By the time you get to your junior or senior year, you will encounter a lot of laws of diminishing returns, which will allow you to take more major classes and fewer general classes.

Being a freshman, I was offered general courses such as Architectural Graphics, Management, Math, as well as Economics. At times, I found it uneasy shuffling my time in these classes. However, it was loving to have the privilege of exploring various subjects which ordinarily, I wouldn't have had the prospect to do. Rushing to declare my major almost cost me. This will be discussed later on here. Though hectic, it remained pleasurable for me to learn from other people's cultures around the globe.

In this vein, never underestimate the level of your ignorance at your first encounter with freedom in the college. Do not waiver. Drive out the motivation from within. Whatsoever you'd become shouldn't be determined by your first experience with life in college. It may be scary, but that notwithstanding, you can still turn out to become pacesetters for posterity.

Since classes were still not taken seriously and with the luxury of time at my disposal, I found it trouble-free to mark virtually all the box during the event of the students' gathering. My eagerness to be sociable by being part of this lively event was superb. Gradually, my life in the college hit a cadence as I ate, studied, and slept.

And before I could think of welcoming spring semester at all, I've found myself rooted in many clubs and I saw myself doing a lot of internships that helped me in my sustenance. With my school having quite a number of extracurricular activities, it turned out to be unproblematic for me to make friends. Nonetheless, the timing of the College can get in the way of your meetings, sporting events, rehearsals on stage, working hours, etc.

The best thing about the College is having the privilege to be yourself and fashion out your natural potentials (acting, singing, drawing, writing, travelling, etc.)

Let me quickly straighten this out. Many times, college timing can appear annoying.

Having to stay up late in the night to do homework wasn't thrilling at all for me, but my heart was fully glued to what I did and everything I learned. The flexibility attached to college, which made students become masters of what they'd become was outstanding to me. You've got to prepare as well for an awesome responsibility. You will be taught how to manage your time too. And when you give it proper planning, you will get to become a success.

For you to survive in a milieu with mammoth of crowd from different parts of the world, you've got to be working hard. After this, you will claim your degree which nobody can revoke from you. When I flashed back to my days in the College as a sophomore, I wished I had the in-depth knowledge of what I'm about to tell you now even before I left for College.

1. Making it to the College is the same as working as a full-time worker

The biggest mistake I made as a prospective sophomore was the thought I nurtured that the College is like secondary school, and that definitely, it will go on smoothly.

Regrettably, I got it all wrong! I had to live in the dorm made available by the College. By implication, I dined, socialised, studied, and hung out at the same place that was another activity entirely. A lot of things that happened in the life of students such as studies, social activities and sporting events will definitely be related to life in the College.

It took me time to acquaint myself with the fact that what I'd be doing would be more than just staying in class to study. There were times when some couple of friends and I had to go out on the field to work on assignments, group study or research works which gave us time also to acclimatise ourselves with the environment.

Most times that I devoted to works in the College were more than 40 hours in just a week. So, get yourself prepared for that kind of task that lay in ambush ahead of you. Brace yourself up for the challenges that come with the transformation you're about to experience now.

2. **Know that extracurricular activities are pertinent**

Of all the things that I found extremely magnificent in the College, knowing that it wasn't all about academics was fun to me. Despite the fact that it wasn't a prerequisite in the academia, many students were actively involved and that alone turned a larger society into a microcosm.

If you embrace extracurricular activities as a freshman, you won't only be taught new skills with an assurance of gaining new experiences in spanking new things; you'll also be strongly involved in an activity, which will at least help you to inflate your network and fashion out friendships that linger forever.

You should also know this for sure that extracurricular activities need your time, commitment and dedication. Thus, it will be unwise should you decide to take part in so many activities. Ensure you do not engulf yourself with the activities. Have this in mind that your studies come first.

3. Never be in a hurry to decide your Major.

Since you're preparing for life in the college as a sophomore, it's essential for you to know that you might not declare your major until your sophomore year has come to an end.

Despite knowing that I should major in Architecture, I opted for Estate management and that really affected me in its own way. You might know what to study, but if you're yet to be specific, like me then, it isn't bad if you don't choose your major on time. One of the benefits of the British/American education is the stress laid on exploration of various fields, which definitely isn't offered anywhere around the globe.

4. Understanding the Social Life of the School's environment

College experience comes with a huge option which is your social life. When I encountered College life as a freshman, the aspect of my social life was quite exhilarating. You need to understand the culture of the society you will school. Having the understanding that British and/or Americans are quite friendly and open-minded to other people has given you an edge. All you need to do is to just key into that; strike up conversation in the park or train station with unfamiliar faces on topics of interest. This will pretty much go a long way to help you get established.

5. Go for part-time jobs at the College

The moment you're set to leave for College; get the understanding that there are a lot of jobs on campus. And you don't have to wake up your mom in the dead of the night when it's not yet mid-semester for reimbursement over an expense to be paid on campus. Remember that one of the freedoms you've got is financial freedom.

It never dawned on me that I'd have the opportunity to really work on campus. My sophomore year had almost run out when the opportunity came. After grabbing it, I never regretted to have done so. Taking up a job relating to my field of study made the job easy for me to do.

When you work, especially at something that has link with your field of study, you'll have an ample opportunity to be familiar with people in your field and in the same vein be paid for the service rendered. Quite a number of Universities possess teaching assistantships with a lot of research chances which are worth checking out. Do not be timid to walk up to that Doctor or Professor in your department. S/he may be your gold mine.

I recollected having to walk up to my supervisor requesting him to make me his research assistant, unknown to me that he'd been wanting to announce same in class the next day. All he did was to put me through the basics of being his helper. Not only did he pay me stipend for my efforts, but also drilled me into understanding more about my academic field. That made this acts as two-way benefits.

6. Be part of the discussion in class

I rose up in one of our Economics classes to defend the American economy one of my colleagues tried to bastardise. That caught a lot by surprise and that act alone attracted attention of many to my side.

Therefore, no matter the outcome of your intellectual contribution, do not hesitate to stand up and contribute to the class discussion. Should you have points to raise or questions to ask, voice out and make your mark right from the first impression. You'll hardly have another privilege to be part of an open discussion with regards to exciting topics with others. *Take the bull by its horns in the class and get endeared to the Professors.*

Welcoming yourself this way will go a long way in leaving long-lasting cologne around you. Maximise your presence in the College and be the catalyst for change there.

Create Successful Studying at College

Late night cramming, finishing assignments in the student lounge on the day they are due, praying for a good essay topic to come your way. Does any of this sound familiar? Yes, these are some of the characteristics of a university education with which many of us are familiar. Part of the university experience is about having great times with friends, growing as a person, and yes some get together! However, let's not forget about the actual "reason" for university in the first place. If you've forgotten I'll remind you! It's about getting a great education, getting high grades, and preparing yourself for the future of your dreams. That's reasonably true isn't it? The reason you came to university was to get an education?

I was lucky enough to get through university with some pretty good marks and options for the future. But, it didn't come easy. I learned the hard way by trial and error to figure out the right combination of study tactics that worked for me.

TIPS FOR #COLLEGELIFE

I wish the same school success for you as well. But not the same hard knocks of trial and error, although some of that is probably unavoidable. It can be much easier to get through university if you have a methodology to follow or even some simple tips to better studying. Even though it may be a bit of a fight to actually get your studying and assignments done, with everything else going on around you, it is worth your while to learn some strategies to help you in this area. The following are some tips for studying that may help you with the studious part of your university career.

Tip #1: Make a decision for yourself to place a high priority on grades. You are the only one that will actually prioritise this. Even though your parents may really nag at you to get your studying and assignments done, ultimately it is up to you. You are the boss of your destiny, not your friends, profs, or parents. Make your residence a place that promotes studying, assignments, and learning. This will help you prioritise school work both at school and at home.

Tip #2: Create a habit of doing something fun and rewarding after studying. Make it a rule that you must get school work done first and play second. Fun time may include going out with friends, chatting on the phone or online with friends, watching a favourite TV program, playing a game, working out, etc.

Tip #3: Schedule time to study and do assignments every day at the same time if you can. Be specific about what time and for how long studying is to take place each day. This promotes studying as a habit and a regularly scheduled activity. We tend to find things easier to do when they have become a routine activity. However, also schedule in time when you will not be doing any homework, such as on Sunday.

Tip #4: Encourage a positive and focused study atmosphere. A good place to study is one with good lighting, a desk and chair, and few or no distractions. This place provides pencils, pens, paper, a stapler, calculator, ear plugs, tissue, highlighters, a computer, and anything else needed for your school work. This helps to avoid time wasted on looking around for each accessory separately.

Tip #5: Make it fun to get good grades. Set positive consequences in place for getting good grades. You want to pay attention to and be focused on the good things you do much more than the bad things you do. It can be easy to get into a habit of being hard on yourself for mistakes of the past. Learn from them, let them go, and move forward into a better future. Notice and celebrate the good things you do, especially getting good grades. Take yourself to a movie, buy yourself your favourite Starbucks treat, or just relax at home. Do whatever will be rewarding for you.

Tip #6: Work on creating new study habits. New habits take approximately 90 days to create. This means that you will need to use willpower and motivation for the first 90 days. After that the habits you have created will be more automatic and come much more easily. The earlier in life you establish healthy habits for yourself the better off you will be in the long run. Good habits not only include studying but also healthy eating, working out, balancing work and play, and being compassionate with yourself and with others.

CHAPTER TWO
HOW TO BE PREPARED AS A FRESHER

Going to college represents an enormous transition and poses numerous challenges. It is an extremely exciting time, but also a time of great change. It represents an almost overnight passage from being a teenager, with limited freedom and responsibility, to becoming an adult with seemingly unlimited freedom and responsibility.

Now, let's get specific. There are many things that students should do BEFORE arriving on campus.

1. Get to know your roommate.

There are few things as important as this. For most, you will usually be sharing a room with a complete and total stranger. Anything you can do during the summer to get to know your roommate is crucial. Sometime in mid-summer, every student will receive their "Housing Packet" which will tell you what residence hall you will be living in and who your roommate(s) will be. It will also give the email and phone number of your new roommate(s). Email them as soon as possible and introduce yourself! Keep the initial email short and sweet, just a simple introduction. After you receive a response you may email again or even pick up the phone and call. But, DO NOT WAIT ... get to know your roommate(s) as soon as possible and definitely BEFORE you go to college.

2. Get to know your college town.

If you are unable to visit your school, do a virtual visit online if your college offers it. Get to know everything you can about your school. But don't stop there: get to know the surrounding area as well. Become as familiar with the area as possible. If everything is new and unknown, it can be very intimidating, so familiarising yourself will help to alleviate some of this and help you get involved with the community. Allow your parents to be a part of this "research" if at all possible. If you don't want your parents to be "hovering" when you head off to college, giving them a sense of comfort about the area you will be living in, will go a long ways to ease their concerns and in turn, take some of the pressure from you!

3. Start networking and forming a community.

SOCIAL MEDIA has done a huge service for universities and college students. It gives every student the opportunity to get to know others that will be going to their same college before they go. On social media, you are able to interact in a virtual community which will make those in-person introductions when you arrive on campus that is much more comfortable. Reach out to other individuals from your area who you will be studying with and start making connections as early as possible.

4. Talk about money with parents.

One of the most useful things you can do before you head off to college is to learn everything you can about finances. Instead of just playing for the rest of the summer, take some time to learn about money. Learn how much work it takes to send you to the college you will be attending. Doing so will help you push yourself to get the most out of the education you will be receiving. What about if you talked with your parents about your desire to understand finances? If during dinner one night you said to your Dad, 'Hey, Dad, I know that college is just around the corner, and I was wondering if you could help me with understanding my finances before I go'. Now, when your Dad regains consciousness, he is going to want to make sure that he heard you right - reassure him that you are serious. I can almost guarantee that he will be more than happy to sit down with you and walk you through Financial Stuff. Plus there is an additional benefit to this: Your parents will see that you are serious about being smart with money, and when you have a problem in college with your finances (note that I said 'when', not 'if'), they will be much more ready and willing to help you figure it all out.

But what should that family 'money conversation' include? What are some of the things that you and your parents can talk through before you head off to college? Keep it simple, and the ideas included below are ones to make sure that you talk about:

1. Finding out one another's expectations

2. Setting up a budget

3. Balancing a checkbook

4. Debit/Credit Cards

5. Prepare for Move-In Day.

Make the trip to college and "Move-In Day" a BIG deal. No matter how busy parents are, this is a once-in-a-lifetime opportunity. Make an event out of moving to college! Do this together and enjoy. Many students think they are ready to move out and do it all on their own. This may be the case, but regardless, it is so important to make this Rite of Passage, moving to college, a family affair. Understand this is a difficult time and last moments for your parents, and be as understanding and accepting of their nagging for a couple more hours. They only want to see you succeed!

If you are a parent, PLEASE don't send your kids off to college -- take them to college, you won't regret it! And if you are the one going off

TIPS FOR #COLLEGELIFE

to college, PLEASE allow your parents to be a part of this. As much as they drive you crazy, they NEED you to let them be a part of this!

Some classes really are "blow off" classes

College is an interesting place. There are people who have no idea what they are going to do in life, and there are people who know exactly what they want to do. John was the latter. John knew that he wanted to do radio or some form of media. That eventually evolved into digital media and social media, but he was always confident about what he wanted to do with his life.

If you are like John, I recommend ignoring some of the required courses the university will shove down your throat. Sure, Biological Anthropology might be interesting, but if you have already decided to stay away from science, why bother paying attention?

John would admit, that there is a satisfaction when four people are pointing to a class he could not care less about, but truth be told, if you know what you want, focus on it. John knew he wanted to be involved in media, so instead of stressing and working hard at required courses that did not interest him, he spent his free time producing media, volunteering at the radio station, and calling play-by-play for basketball games.

However, if you have no idea what you want in life, pay attention in those courses. So long as you have not ruled out the broad subject matter, listen and engage, you might find a gem that will be your calling.

Engage

Sitting in a classroom and taking notes is not learning. Memorising information and spitting it out on an exam, is not learning. Unfortunately, in many ways this is the sad state of our "higher education." In my four years I've come across plenty of professors that are more concerned about their research than educating the people paying for their research.

The fact is, some professors are just as lazy and disengaged as you are. The best professors I've had cared about the subject matter and cared that we learned it. Two of my most memorable professors were in my freshman year. One taught a lecture on statistics. It was a required course; he knew most people would not be interested. But his magic was he made us interested. Instead of standing at the front of the room and lecturing, he would take the first ten minutes of each class and walk around with a microphone and ask students about their weekend or about the course material.

It was a fantastic way to take a 200 person lecture, and make it feel small. Furthermore, it broke that "fourth wall" between the professor and the students. All too often professors teach like theater actors putting on a show and reading from a hazily memorised script. Instead this professor was human with us, and in turn we were more attentive and interested in the subject.

My second favorite professor taught a small writing class my freshman year. He never lectured, instead he listened. That was his magic. He would throw out a topic and listen to us talk to one another. He would prod, poke, and play devil's advocate, but mostly he would listen and make sure the conversation stayed on course. This led to fantastic discussions which resulted in even better papers from the students.

In short, the best professors you'll have will be ones that listen to you instead of themselves. You might be comfortable only taking notes in a 300 person lecture, but don't expect it to pay dividends when it comes to actually learning something.

5. Your professor does not speak the word of God

TIPS FOR #COLLEGELIFE

In some respects, professors live in a bubble. They are surrounded by incredibly smart academics studying and teaching very specific topics, and sometimes it is hard to see the forest through the trees.

When everyone around you believes something, it is human nature to assume that the majority feel that way. When you are surrounded by incredibly bright people and they all say the same thing, it is human nature to assume it is true.

Oftentimes it is not.

I spent my four years as a minority on campus; I was a conservative. Even more frightening for the academic crowd, I was an educated conservative. The horror!

I came across plenty of professors that tried to teach their opinions as if they were verified and peer edited facts. And when they did, I called them out on it. But it does not have to be about politics and it does not have to be that vocal.

Professors are human, they will make mistakes, and sometimes they will either accidentally or purposefully try to teach you something that does not quite pass the sniff test. If you notice this, say something. Again, engagement is the best way to learn, and fact checking your professors is oftentimes the best form of engagement.

Do what you love and do lots of it

At one point during Henry's College life, He was juggling six jobs at once. Yeah, six. Granted not all of them were 15 or even 10 hours a week, but he legally had six different employers. On top of that he had a full time class schedule and, ya know, a life.

During a recent job interview he was asked how he managed to handle so much during his college career. His answer was twofold. One, he found the best way to stay on task was to have so much to do, you have no other choice. If he mismanaged even one hour of his time, he could seriously get behind. And two, everything he did he loved doing.

Henry was lucky enough to find jobs that fit into his major and his interests. He wasn't washing dishes at a dorm cafeteria, He was designing websites, working on social media, and prepping to call play-by-play for basketball games. He sought out jobs that He would want to work at and that would further his education. There's no reason you can't do the same.

If you need a college job, check with your school first. See if there are any paid internships or people on campus hiring. If you are attending a big school I guarantee there are opportunities in the field you are interested in. Procrastination sets in when you dread doing work. However, you can avoid the nagging urge to shirk responsibilities by surrounding yourself with work and tasks that you enjoy. Life is too short, and your college career is too short, to waste time on stuff you are not passionate about.

Be passionate about something

It is hard to surround yourself with tasks you are passionate about if you have no passion. College is an opportunity to find that passion. Whether it be animals, helping inner city children, or curling (yes the Olympic sport) I'm sure you can find other likeminded passionate people on campus to interact with.

And I know it is a cliché but, find your passion and make it a career. If you really love animals, why be a financial planner? College is your opportunity to do what you love. It is also an opportunity to explore and find what you love. You have a 22-year window to be a one dimensional passionless human, find your passion in college and ride it for the rest of your life.

Savor it

Sharon only graduated from college a week ago, but her biggest regret so far was that she moved too fast. She can honestly say that college was the quickest four years of her life. It was like the sole traffic light in a small country town, blink and it is gone. For all the pain, stress, and headaches you will endure, you will also experience joy, happiness, and amazing people. There's no need to rush through that.

Walk slowly. Eat slowly. Enjoy slowly. Do not rush to get to class, leave five minutes early and enjoy the walk. Don't waste a beautiful Saturday evening, go find a lake and stare at it. College is the last four years of your life that are bound to education. The last four years subsidised by your parents. The last four years that you can skip class and enjoy the unseasonably warm weather. Don't forget to savor that.

As Sharon was flipping through the senior edition of her secondary school newspaper she came across the back page. This page was dedicated to the seniors on the staff. They had picked quotes that meant something, inside jokes that they adored, and advice that they had for others.

Sharon's advice was, "get off your lazy sit and do something. Secondary school is fun when you sit back and watch, but it is exhilarating when you are the one being watched."

Sharon still believe that, although she will replace "secondary" with "life." Her entire life is too short to just sit back and watch. Just like college or secondary school, life is more fulfilling, gratifying, and exhilarating if you are the one other people are watching.

Be Responsible, Manage Yourselves

Once you're in University, majority of you will be adult age by then and will be treated as one. As adults, it comes with a ton of responsibilities.

Most importantly, it is the responsibility you have to yourself.

University is a transitional phase. Some just entered straight from secondary school and still need a lot of help. Some are still struggling in University even a few years after secondary school. Everyone has their own pace with how they grasp at things. And that's fine too. But University is also the perfect time to start picking up the little things so that bit by bit you can become more independent and successful without having to rely on so much help from others.

I'm talking about the responsibility of knowing what the different processes at your University are that you're applying for, checking out the deadlines to specific things, being careful and reading the forms you need to fill out and sign, reading all the notifications and emails you get from school, planning accordingly so your schedule doesn't go all over the place...

And much more.

While all the things I just listed might sound a lot, when you look at it, it's not really that scary. A lot of these things are pretty simple to do and can be taken care of by yourselves. Some of these things may require maybe extra help, but these things shouldn't have to be managed by someone else completely for you.

It is your responsibility to check for yourself that you have everything you need to be fully prepared before classes starts.

After all, you'll be held accountable for stuff related to your College process because it is Your College life and how more important can it get than that? Being on top of things is the key to success.

Manage yourself well and you'll succeed.

Manage yourself horribly, and you only have yourself to blame.

Don't rely on others to help you a 100% with everything. Because no matter what's been provided to help you through College, no one's truly responsible to keep you continuously rolling on semester after semester, as much as yourselves.

Only you have that capability to seek your own benefit a 110% in life and others around you. Only you truly know what you yourselves want to do in life, and it's your life on the line and those decisions that you make are what shape Your life.

And that's your greatest responsibility: yourselves.

Apply for Stuff Early

1. Packed Days: If you want to wait until the last minute to get things settled for the semester, be aware that others may do the same thing too, which, results in a Very long waiting line. First week of school is pretty busy at the major offices -like admissions, financial aid, etc. Take note of the last week of the semester too, cause that's when people feel the upcoming semester right

around the corner and want to get everything done and out of the way too.

2. Process May Take a Long Time. Don't expect things to happen right away just because you apply to them. There are a lot of things to factor in or check at, so it can take quite some time to process. Applying for something a few weeks before the semester starts when the process can take a Really long time, that can last longer than just a few weeks will leave you unprepared for when College hits the first day. Or, if something is an issue and the process gets delayed, it might make you miss a certain deadline for whatever you're applying too.

3. Find & Correct Mistakes Early: If you apply or at least start an application early, you will have more time to look over your mistakes before you submit it. Giving you some leeway and room in case the things you submitted also have something that comes up and there's a delay in the process or there's something that you need to fix.

4. Appointments: If you need to make an appointment with a counsellor or such, you can do schedule appointments when you like, but make sure you Do Not Delay Making appointments. If you really need an appointment

for something academic, and you wait 'til the busiest time of the semester (again first week, last week...), you may not be able to get the time slot you wanted.

Bottom Line: Not only does applying for things early gives you a cushion against time if things go wrong, but you'll be more prepared.

All About That Food

Bring your own Food/Lunch.

1. Campus food is expensive. Bringing your own food/lunch not only saves you money. You get a choice to bring healthier food if all your campus food provides is unhealthy food. And campus food may not be the best to eat either. At Sharon's campus, She has gotten queasy from eating one of the food areas there twice. So yeah.

2. The Unpredictability of Looking for Food Off Campus, Especially Nearby: As a person who pretty much just stays on campus and then go home, maybe this is not the best advice I can give you. But what I do know is that I would be worried about the unpredictability: food places nearby may be great or taste horrible, may be cheap or may be expensive. Or maybe, like the university where Sharon is at, it isn't really that safe to take a stroll in the areas outside of her campus, even if it's a few blocks away - at least

TIPS FOR #COLLEGELIFE

that's the reputation she has come to hear of and it is kind of a...which from what she has seen kind of seems a bit true from the university she is attending at.

So to stay safe, bring your own food/lunch might be better.

Of course, if you're really found tons of awesome nearby food places, and you can be able to travel off campus, and you're not really worried for safety, by all means go for it if you want to! :D

3. Microwaves – if your campus has a microwave, please cover your stuff so that your lunch does not spray all over the place inside the microwave. Or so that nasty stuff left over inside the microwave's ceiling by someone else does not get into your lunch contents.

Avoid Procrastination

Don't procrastinate.

University...well once the stuff starts rolling, it really does start rolling. Until you have a humongous snowball the size of a car chasing you down the hill.

If you keep procrastinating, that habit might bleed to other areas of your life as well - like delaying to fix things, goals, tasks in career, etc....until you turn around and look at your life Aw, I've been doing it wrong.

Avoiding to do certain things now isn't going to get you very far. Because as much as you will like to avoid it forever, you still are going to have to do it. You might as just well get it over with.

And even if you only procrastinate only on your education....well it can lead to sleepless nights that impact your health, it can slow you down on your courses and maybe even getting out with your education faster, etc.

It's kind of hard for a lot of students to not procrastinate. And I'm pretty sure a lot of you do it at some point or another. Just don't make it into a bad habit. And try to work on it as much as possible.

Studying Tips

1. Music. Sharon can't for the life of her just listen to any music she likes without getting distracted. She daydreams a ton and then minutes disappear to half an hour to an hour...

Other times she YouTubes her music then get distracted with a bunch of other videos from there and it just leads to mayhem distraction....

So...

So she keeps certain types of music on repeat, and even if she wants to change it, she didn't. Sounds boring and sometimes the music she listens to just doesn't fit what she is daydreaming too when she is thinking of scriptures and songs...but if it helps you focus and calm down, then do it.

Plus, it's almost like burning a CD into her mind too! And after burning said song into her mind after so many repeats, now she can carry it offline when she doesn't have Wi-Fi and wish to study! Automatically play in the back of her head...Isn't that great? Lol, joking....sorta...

If it helps, Sharon likes to listen to Hill songs music and videos. It's pretty happy vibe when you only listen to the music so it doesn't fit your daydreaming of epic battles and whatnot...but it sure gives a slighter boost in feeling slightly more energetic to finish

2. 15 minute Breaks. If you're definitely starting to get a little irritated or frustrated with studying on a certain subject or your eyes start to feel really tired from looking at it so long while your brain can't really digest the stuff in front...break. Just take a calm break. Your mind sound like it's about to explode.

You can run, walk around (which is what I did on campus and at home), do something different, rest, close your eyes for a bit, anything that can let you relax and cool down.

Sometimes a little distraction is nice.

But don't abuse your breaks though! Make sure not to go overboard and let the breaks lead on to longer than an hour....otherwise....it's pointless. You have just sunken yourself once again into the woeful pit of distraction. :/

3. Group Study Only If it Helps

It helps if everyone's getting focused on the subject. It doesn't help if group members and yourself start talking about other subjects and getting carried away. And if you're more of a solo learner, maybe it's not the best way to study. I did prefer to study at least by myself if and when I could do it right before the test.

CHAPTER THREE
IMPORTANT ORIENTATION OF A FRESHER

As a fresher you need proper orientation on student's life in the college, so these part of the orientation is the mandatory part of your experience, That will motivate you as a fresher.

THINGS THAT WILL MOTIVATE YOU;

1. Identity is destiny:

Who am I? Who do I desire to become? For what reason am I in college in the first place?

2. Pinpoint college students purpose:

To begin strong and stay the course, a successful college student needs to have a powerful vision of his or her future. If it is not quite crystal clear initially, that is o.k., as vision is progressive as it is passionately and purposefully pursued continually. Take a broad brush of classes if you are unsure what path you should take. This will help you get a good taste of everything college has to offer you before making any big life-changing decisions.

3. Beyond books and school work, how will I structure my life:

Depending upon college students passion and purpose, you may want to pursue a variety of extra-curricular activities. Joining student fellowships is a wonderful way to make friends and align with an established organisation on campus through whom you can do charitable work and let your voice be heard. If this appeals to you, evaluate the mission statement of each one.

Student associations and organisations on most college campuses are many, each possessing a different focus and objective. Get acquainted with your student union, student government, and student fellowship executives. As you become acquainted with these various organisations and associations on campus, attend some "meet and greet" sessions early in the year or whenever possible to familiarise yourself with whatever groups spark an interest and seem to suit your personal preference. Look for opportunities to get involved if you feel comfortable, as it is a great way to meet other people!

Keep in mind you don't want to stretch yourself thin by being over committed. Therefore be wise to stay focused on your primary purpose for attending college after which you can choose a complimentary group or professional student group organisation with whom to align yourself.

Remember also to eat healthy, get plenty of sleep, and exercise regularly. Many college students forget to do so and later suffer when their immune systems are run down by winter. Think long-term and prepare to go the distance and finish your college studies strong all year round.

4. Proximity is key to fulfilling your destiny:

Sit at the front of class whenever possible to be sure to absorb all vital class information and test material. It is also harder to get distracted when you sit towards the front. Less talking and disturbances occur in the front of the classroom. Always respect and befriend professors as much as possible, even if you don't always fully agree with them. At the very least respect their position, remembering they will be grading you and hold the keys to your academic progress and ultimately your future on your course. Professors will be more likely to help and make time for you if you pay attention during their classes.

5. Maintain close relationships with your family:

If you only can stay in touch with your family by phone, make the effort and do so. Since your parents may be financing or helping you finance some part of your education and expenses, the least you can do is check in periodically on a bi-weekly basis and give them an update as to your academic progress and life. Make sure to discuss beforehand your family's expectations for communications, so no one ends up hurt.

Certainly if you were making a substantial financial investment in someone's future you would want the same decency and courtesy to be shown you. Therefore be appreciative, courteous, and respectful toward your parents to further endear them to you and build a supportive bond, which in turn will serve you well throughout the course of your life.

6. Be proactive in pursuing and launching your career, while you are yet still in college:

Rather than sitting back and waiting for a resume alone (which usually ends up in a stack of paper) to produce your desirable results professionally, take the initiative to make things happen for yourself. Visit your college career center and begin reviewing various internships in your field that are available to provide you further professional development. Even if these internships don't pay you, the professional experience and knowledge you will gain will be priceless.

If no internships turn up for you, consider launching your own business as an entrepreneur. Providing a product or service is essential business in its simplest form. How can you serve people with your time, talent, and expertise? Consider ways you can serve the administration at your own college and University campus.

If necessary, begin serving people for free to get them to recognise and discover your value to them. When you add value, you will always immediately become valuable. Once you have proven yourself, you can set your price and negotiate a pay raise or launch your own business. Make sure to balance the time spent on your business with your academic studies.

7. Be patient with yourself as you evolve and your career comes into clear focus:

Life and professional development is not done in a microwave. Give yourself some time to evolve and go through the discovery process. As you sample various courses, you will discover in college what you like and dislike; what fits you and what is not you. Don't try to rework or remake yourself to fit something you are not.

Be authentic and true to yourself. As you do, your own uniqueness and difference will emerge. As you delight in and continually develop the genius within, your own success and leadership capacities will emerge and begin to shine.

Keep a childlike heart while pursuing academic and professional life. Remain curious, carefree, fun, but remain simultaneously professional and courteous. As you show yourself friendly and have fun while you get the college schoolwork done, good things and new skills will be developed in you.

CHAPTER FOUR
TIPS FOR INCOMING FRESHERS

Find an on-campus dormitory to live in if one is not already assigned to you. This is one of the most essential things a college freshman should do. Attempt at least to do so for the first year or two of college. Alright, maybe college dorms may not have that much appeal; after all dorm buildings have that reputation of being old and musty smelling with communal bathrooms and showers that are far cry from mom's bathroom at home; but being forced to live with twenty or fifty other students in a single building is essential to your first year social life.

- The friends that you meet during your first few months may become some of the friends that will stay with you all your life. There are endless activities and groups and dorm activities and the list go on. But really, it's a freshman dorm so all the other kids that are in that building are like you: fresh out of secondary school and trying to figure out what college life is. And believe me, it's more fun figuring out the ropes when you have others to figure it out with. The people you are going to be going to classes with live there, so make connections, start study groups, and succeed together!

- Don't play hooky. Going to college is not just about the activities and the friends and the delicious independence. You went to college to study. When it comes to handling coursework or classes, you can get advice a dime a dozen, but the best and easiest thing that you can do to stay on top of your studies and grades is to go to class.

- Pay attention to schedule making. That's what they have freshman advisers for. Because working on your schedule is just as important as the courses you are taking. If you know that an eight a.m class is torture for you, it is better to switch to a class on the ten a.m schedule, should there be any. This will help prevent you from skipping classes or falling asleep and missing valuable information.

- Come clean about your professor's expectations of you as a student. These days, when everything can be posted and accessed online, professors simply post the syllabus online and the topics for discussion the next class and post the assignments and expect that everything will be handed in by the next class. Or that you would have read through the posted course work. It is therefore your responsibility to keep up and hand everything on time and be ready all the time. Your parents wouldn't be around reminding you about homework. How your stint as a college student turns out is entirely up to you. Professors will not be as lenient as they were in years prior, so do not expect them to let you make up missed coursework. It is vital that you stay organised and ahead of the curve.

- Find a study spot for you to spend those times where you can just focus on the assignments that need to be done and read those books you paid a heck of a lot for. Make sure though, that the study spot is quiet and there won't be distractions that can make you forget about that chapter you're supposed to be brushing up on. Find the study strategy that works for you. Whether that is making flashcards, re-writing notes, or repeating lessons aloud, find whatever works best for you and stick with it!

- Have Fun. Most important of all, enjoy college life. See it as an opportunity to discover your talents, seek knowledge and enjoy the company of good friends and great professors.

- Going to college should be a balance of both hard work and fun. You should and you will know when to get serious about your studies and when to just lie back, put your feet up and congratulate yourself for every job well done. Before you know it, you have survived your freshman year with flying colours and graduation is just around the corner.

CHAPTER FIVE
HOW TO SURVIVE YOUR FRESHMAN YEAR

Going to University will change your life and it will change who you are as a person. The things you'll see and do, the people you'll meet, and the life lessons you'll learn will be both enriching and humbling. It is my hope that through this guide, you'll walk away from your academic career in three, four or even five years time with degree in hand and tons of positive life experience under your belt. Here are my top 10 tips for surviving your freshmen year at University!!

Top 10 Tips on How to Survive Your Freshman Year at University

As a sophomore who has been through first year two times (okay maybe it was three...), I like to think I'm an authority on the subject of what works and what doesn't when it comes to making it through your freshman year with GPA and dignity intact.

Tip #1 - GO TO CLASS!

I can't emphasise this one enough even if it should be common sense. Going into my first year at University, I had an academic ego the size of Texas. I graduated secondary school with a very high average and was one of those kids who didn't have to do much rigorous homework or study to get those high grades, it just came naturally. Maybe it's the shock of being on your own for the first time or maybe it's the fact that University professors will not and do not cuddle you into getting your work done or showing up for class but College is much more difficult than secondary school. I believed I could use the material on the websites in combination with the assigned text book and breeze through without ever attending class. I was wrong. Life outside of campus has distractions. If you don't have the discipline to actually work from home and ignore the distractions, you'll fail. Going to class is the message you need everyday to keep your mind centred on what you're actually at University for; an education. So no matter what, no matter how awesome the get together was last night, get out of bed and get to class..

Tip #2 - Balance Your Academic Time With Your Social Time

If you're going out 4 nights per week and assuming the University student stereotype, then you had better be using the other 3 nights of the week for cramming, assignments, lab reports, and general upkeep on your classes. You cannot fall into the downward spiral that so many others do. Imagine yourself 4 years from this moment. Will you be happiest with a degree, being done school FOREVER and embarking on your career? Or, will you be happiest with memories of the time you wasted? With everything you do during your time at University, always keep your education in the back of your mind and make decisions with some maturity.

Tip #3 - Do the assignments!

This should be a no-brainer. Just like in secondary school when the teacher gave you an assignment, you did it. The only catch was that in secondary school the assignments were graded and critiqued. In University many assignments are OPTIONAL. Yes that's right, optional. As in, not for grades, assessment, or critiquing of any sort. Do them anyway. Up until this point this is how you've learned. It's ingrained into your head that doing assignments is the way you understand new ideas and subjects. So don't break the cycle now, just do them and know it'll pay off later when it comes to exam time.

Tip #4 - Meet People

As you progress through your degree program you'll need people you can depend on for homework questions, occasional answers to questions you have, and general peer support. Go to events and get togethers put on by your College so you can meet people with the same academic interests and classes as you. Many connections you make in your first couple of years at University will be lifelong and once you all graduate the professional connections will be invaluable. Also, don't forget to personally introduce yourself to your professors. Many "keener" students use this trick to encourage themselves to attend lectures and do well in the class. If you feel you "know" the teacher, you'll want to perform well in their class so you don't feel like you disappointed them.

Tip #5 - Take Classes You Enjoy

Most degree programs have openings for electives. Electives are slots in your degree that you can fill with just about anything! For example, you're taking a commerce degree but you love to travel to Central America. Fill in one of those elective slots with a Spanish class. It'll go towards your degree and you'll have another language you can lean on for the rest of your life! This also has the added benefit of having a class in your schedule that you actually enjoy going to. There's a HUGE difference between classes you don't enjoy and classes you do, and your performance in it will show.

Tip #6 - Spend Your Money Wisely

Unless you come from a wealthy family, money will likely be scarce throughout your 4 years of post-secondary education. Most students require loans of some kind, either private or government. Just because you have access to a whole pile of money doesn't mean it's time to book a £3000 spring break trip to the Bahamas. Budget your money and make it last as far as you can. The stress that comes with living month-to-month can have a large impact on your overall level of happiness which will affect your performance academically. If you have enough spare time, consider getting a part-time job just to offset the costs of living a University student's life. Even if your expenses are reasonable, an income will keep your debt down making your transition from student to professional upon graduation much, much more enjoyable.

Tip #7 - Lean on Your Family

Family will always be there for you so make sure you stay in touch as much as you can. Whether it's through frequent visits or care packages through the mail, your parents and family will support you the whole way through. Talking with and seeing your family keeps you connected to the life you left behind and subconsciously this will do wonders for your stress and confidence levels. When times get tough, don't hesitate to call home for whatever kind of support it is that you need as your family is often the one thing in life you can count on to always be there for you.

Tip #8 - Choose the Right Field of Study

So many students choose their degree program according to what their family expects or how much money they will make after graduating. This is not a good idea. Choose a program that suits your strengths and most importantly your interests. The worst possible thing you can do is begin a program and end up hating it at the halfway point. You'll be miserable and you'll likely end up failing. Do your research prior to going to University and find the program that is right for you. If you can't decide, narrow your choices down to 2 or 3. Find an entire year's worth of classes that each program has in common so that at the end of your first year you're able to enter whichever program you've found to interest you the most.

Tip #9 - Begin Your Exam Studying at Least One Week Prior to Exam Day

This tip is something very few students seem able to do. Personally I seem to perform well by cramming everything in the night before. It's stressful, tiring, and if you can't optimize your study time and study according to a priority list then you really need to begin exam review several days before the exam. Any upper-year student will tell you that small review sessions with practice questions each day is the best way to prepare. However anyone in a tough degree program will often say this is not possible due to major time constraints nearing the end of a semester. Everyone is different and has to find a study process that works for them but almost anyone who is successful in post-secondary level schooling will tell you that the more time you use for studying prior to an exam, the easier it will be.

Tip #10 - Do Whatever it Takes

If you find yourself falling behind or struggling to understand major aspects of your classes, you have to step up your effort. Some classes are just incredibly hard and the entire class will struggle through it but most are doable with even an average effort put forth. Attend other sections if your schedule allows, lookup resources on the internet, meet with your professor to discuss your difficulties, or find a tutor or study group. It eats up a lot of your spare time but you have to remember each class is only four months long so it's a small price to pay to be one small step closer to graduation.

CHAPTER SIX
HOW TO MAKE USE OF YOUR TIME IN THE COLLEGE

It's one of the greatest times in life. When do any of us ever get to hang out with hundreds of friends for four, five...dare I say...six years? It's like going to camp. Except they give you homework and you have to read 800 pages a night.

Here are some ways that I believe you could not only make the most of your time in college, but really, really enjoy it and succeed at it - here's what Is important;

1. Meet people.

One day you'll walk across a stage, and a very smart looking man or woman in a really nice, long, black gown will hand you a piece of paper that says "Bachelor" (even if you're a girl!) on it. You'll graduate from university. Do you know what you'll remember most?

TIPS FOR #COLLEGELIFE

The relationships you've made with the people walking across the stage with you.

My advice is to meet everyone you can. Be friendly. Smile. Talk to people (not in class...that could be dangerous). Go to fellowships where people hang out and hang out with them. Your friends are what makes college special.

Some day you'll come back to campus as an alumni and the place will feel weird. It will feel different. That's because all of the people that you were friends with during your college years aren't there. It's the same college, but different people. It's the people that make your experience unique. You are going to make friends that you'll have for the rest of your life. If nothing else use College to make connections with people that will be at your side for the rest of your life

My friend who is a professor (yes...he's smarter than me) is a good friend that I went to college all four years with. It's been a great relationship for all this time. I don't know of any other place you create these types of relationships at this age. So get out there. Get busy meeting people and sharing life.

2. Talk to your professors.

This one continues on with the theme of number 1. Go ahead and do everything you can to meet your professors. Make an appointment with them as soon as it is possible in their schedule. I have discovered that I learned so much more from a professor when I had some kind of personal relationship with them.

Professors are people too, respect their time and make sure you communicate clearly with them. Don't waste their time with excuses for not doing the work or simply not showing up in class. The goal here is to establish some type of relationship no matter how small. Some of these professors teach thousands of students, and making a connection with them helps you stand out from all the rest.

I once heard a story about a secondary school senior that wants to get into university. He's enamored with the writings of a certain professor there. When he finally has the chance to meet the professor and sit down and talk with him, it changes his entire perspective. While those types of conversations might be rare in your experience because you go in no small

College - seek them out anyway! They'll be some of the best memories you take from your time in college, and having a strong connection with your professor could open up job opportunities later on in life.

3. If you need help ask for it.

One of the reasons you're in college is because you don't know everything. If you can learn to admit that, you'll be ahead of most first-year students at your school.

Independence messes up most teenagers in that they want to do everything by themselves without another person's valuable help. So when a moment comes when they can't do something or don't know something, there's an inner struggle. I encourage you to put the pride aside and ask for help.

If you need help in class, get a tutor. If you need directions to the help aid office, ask for them. If you don't know how to complete an application for an internship, look for someone who does.

Your school will have people that can proofread your papers, help you learn how to do your laundry the right way, and even give you some good advice on how to stay in shape (because we all need our health!).

Look at it this way: You will become smarter if you ask for help when you need it. If you don't ask...you'll remain ignorant. I'm not advocating that you shouldn't try to find things out on your own. But there comes a time where you'll discover that learning happens better in the context of "we" and not just "me." And you might also discover that the best way to meet people is to simply ask, "Hi, would you mind giving me a hand with this?"

4. Get some sleep.

One thing that you have in common with every other person in the world is that each person needs to sleep. If you don't get enough sleep, nasty things could start happening to your mind and body. I know this is difficult to hear, and I'm probably beginning to sound a bit parental by saying this, but go to bed.

I've pulled my share of all-nighters. I've had to study, cram, write, and just get it done. I've also stayed up too late because the convo with Helen kept getting interesting... Either way, it messed me up for the next day and didn't allow me to function to the best of my abilities in class or other events. My body had to play catch up. I wasn't sharp. If you string enough late nights together, you are not going to be the learning machine that you need to be.

I know you're young and invincible. But sleep is so necessary. I once heard that a night of sleep deprivation is like being mentally impaired by the proper blood-drink level. When you don't get adequate sleep, your body ages faster, and puts you at risk for numerous other ailments, like heart diseases. Sleep also helps to relieve stress...so if you're stressed out - you may simply need a good nap.

Ultimately, getting enough sleep is a matter of prioritisation. Just because you CAN stay up, doesn't mean you SHOULD stay up. You need to be mature enough to know when you need to get some sleep so that you can be an effective college student, and make the most of your time there.

5. Get organised.

You need a plan to accomplish all of the things that are required of you in college. It is incredibly easy to start living from event to event, assignment to assignment when you're neck deep into your semester.

My number one piece of advice for getting organised - get a calendar and stick to it, live by it, and look at it everyday. Update it regularly. Now there's lots of types of calendars out there. I like to use Google Calendar. It's online and I can access it from anywhere. Since I spend a fair bit of time on the computer, it's always handy. Plus, I've got it linked up to my email and the datebook software on my Palm Treo. But that's my way. I made a choice one day that Google Calendar was going to be MY calendar. You've got to decide and stick with it.

Some universities will provide you with a paper-based calendar like a planner. This may include dates of important events for your college, key deadlines, and class schedules. If you are pen & paper minded, this may be the route for you. I also recommend the Moleskine planner. It's smaller and easier to carry. In present-day's world, there are thousands of ways to stay organised and ahead of the game, find your system and keep to it to be successful!

Once you've chosen your calendar, you need to get busy putting EVERYTHING into it. That's right. Put every assignment, every deadline, every part of your extensive activity commitments. Remember, you don't want to be surprised. It's a horrible feeling to realise that you had a vital paper due yesterday. At the beginning of each semester, sit down with all of your syllabi and fill in that calendar. Set reminders a few days before big projects come due. This will also help you to see when you will have difficult weeks with lots of obligations so you can get cracking ahead of time.

Now that you've chosen a calendar, put all your information in it, you've got to manage it. At the start of each week, look over the week ahead. KNOW WHAT'S COMING! If you only look at each day as it arrives, you'll miss opportunities to be excellent, as working on a paper or project over a couple of days will yield better results than starting it the night before. The more prepared you are, the better.

That's the beauty of being organised. It creates space for you to do your best work. You know when something is coming and you make the appropriate time to do your best.

6. Have fun.

This is one of the best parts of the college. You are going to have a ton of fun...especially if you follow the other pieces of advice in this book. College is one of the most fun experiences you will ever have. You are living with a lot of other like-minded people who are in the same situation that you're in. It's like Survivor (especially in the school cafeteria), but no one gets voted off the island.

I laughed a lot in college. I liked to hang around people who love what I love and stand for, who made me laugh and didn't take themselves so seriously. There were lots of fellowship events to attend. My buddies and I would take some great roadtrips during the breaks. There is a lot of freedom to do a lot of great things while you're in college. I chose to have as much fun as was humanly possible.

The other benefit of having fun is that it makes incredible memories. I can remember some phenomenal pranks that have become lore at the college I attended (I won't say what it is, or my own level of involvement because the statute of limitations has yet to expire).

Also, I don't want you to get the impression that all of the fun occurred outside of the classroom. When you discover what your unique strengths are then you can land in a significant that falls in line with your passions, learning becomes tremendously fun. I can remember projects and classes that I really enjoyed and looked forward to them. I think there were some professors who really made learning fun.

I guess with any aspect of college you can make the choice to have fun or to stress out. I encourage you to choose fun when time permits - even in the midst of hard work. Just make sure not to sacrifice your grades because you were having too good of a time to study!

7. Get involved.

During the first semester of the college, I joined a scripture union. I had to do some really engaging scripture studies and drama stuff in my subgroup (I have fond memories of playlets acted, I remember someone saying "thank you, ma, may I have another." and we all burst out laughing it wasn't even that funny, but the ambience just called for it) Experiences like this changed my entire college experience. When you arrive on campus, there will be a lot of ways that you can get involved in college besides going to class.

Your college has multiple organisations that are centred around spiritual, social or academic themes. There are clubs and councils that are always looking for new members. You may have a knack for student leadership and I encourage you to jump in and apply for those positions. It has been proven that those students who get involved in extracurricular activities have a better college experience. They also have what it takes to handle life experiences, not to mention student government position which looks great when applying for a job later on.

8. Handle money wisely now.

Right off the bat I must tell you - watch out for credit cards. It is the easiest thing in the world, to get suckered into a credit card offer and start charging things on the plastic. Here's the catch - you have to pay it all back - with interest.

My advice to you is to avoid the credit card route at all costs while you're in school. I know that it's probably unavoidable for some, so just use them for emergency purposes. Get a card with a LOW limit. Pay those things off every month. If you find you can't do that, then you shouldn't be using them. Most college students leave college with debt. There's the necessary kind that comes from student loans.

With the money you do actually have, I think it's wise to learn how to budget. Start a savings account. Invest in shares if you know how. Learn how to balance your checkbook and do that every month. Bounced checks are no fun. The goal here is to live within your means. You may not have as much as other students. That's alright. You are a college student and you're supposed to live within your means, within the financial boundary that has been drawn, and when God sees that you have been faithful within your radius he enlarges it and not only does he enlarges it but he gives you true riches.

TIPS FOR #COLLEGELIFE

If you are in desperate need, make it known to God. God is our Father. He loves us much more than our earthly parents do. My father looked after me from when I was born to the day I got married, without getting anything back. The little gifts and birthday cards I brought him on those special occasions were of course out of what he had given me, and expected nothing really from me in return, till I finished college; even after that, he continued to support me till I got a job and got married.

It is in that same way God cares for all His children. Even birds and animals are fed by Him, and hardly any of them die because of hunger. Yes, people feed them; but those birds and animals don't just sit lazily, like most students do, waiting for their food while playing games. The animals actually go out of their nests and lairs to look for their food, with an absolute assurance that there's something out there each day.

God is Father to all, and regardless of what you do He gives sunshine, oxygen, rain, etc. and other basic needs to all, whether you love Him or not.

In Dubai and the Arab countries, most of the pets are tigers and living lions. Lions! Yet

TIPS FOR #COLLEGELIFE

they provide for those animal's basic needs and feed them every day – just to show you how they provide for animals. You can imagine how much will be needed to feed a lion to satisfaction. Parents don't say, "Because you are naughty, or do bad stuff, you will not eat or be given your basic needs." It's the same with God. He provides for all. He who gives the birds and animals their daily needs will also supply your NEEDS

You can also go to your college's career center. They typically have a listing of odd jobs that students can do to get some extra income. Another thing you can do is to benefit from the ability to share rather than own. You don't have to personally have everything, just know some of the people that do. When you live in a dorm, you begin to understand how easy it is to share. I remember that I cooked beans better in my roommate's pressure cooker than she did. Don't be a mooch. But learn to share what you have with others and you'll find that they're more willing to share what they have with you.

If you spend less money than you bring in...you'll be in good shape.

9. Learn to write well.

One of the lessons I've learned from Scott Ginsberg is that "writing is the basis of all wealth." I think he's on to something there. I would add that writing is the basis of your success in college. While you are a college student, you will read A LOT. But you will also be required to write A LOT. Your writing skills are a KEY factor in how your work will be perceived by a professor.

You can have the best content in the world, but if you aren't able to deliver that through good writing, your work will get lost in translation. I am surprised how many college students can't spell, don't know how to structure a sentence properly, and use poor grammar. If you struggle with writing, then I encourage you to re-read #3. You must get this one down. Meet with tutors to help you work on structure and vocab; this will help your papers flow more efficiently.

One of the reasons that we started the tuition centre (TCEC) is to help students become better communicators. If you can write better, your work will be better. If your work is better, your grades will be better. I realise that you may be the best person in your class at text messaging...but those little acronyms usually don't hold up too well under a professor's scrutiny.

Along with writing, I would encourage you to practice fast typing. The computer is here to stay and if you are typing with two fingers, you're wasting time. I think that you should work to be able to type at least 60 words a minute. Faster would be even better. Can you type without looking at the keyboard? This is a skill that won't only benefit you in college, but in the workforce as well.

One final note on writing well is in regards to proofreading. Please don't type out a paper and print it out and turn it in. Think in terms of drafts. If you turn a first draft into a professor, he or she will know that it's a first draft. This post that what I'm writing won't be published until the third or fourth draft. It would be even better if you could get someone else to proofread your work. That person will probably catch mistakes that you can't see.

10. Get out of the country you're in.

This is an idea that is becoming more and more realistic in our day and age. At different Universities, opportunities to study abroad are growing each year. Universities also offer short-term mission opportunities to other countries. There are so many ways for students to experience other cultures.

Our world is becoming more globally focused. In some ways it's shrinking. Companies are branching out across national boundaries. Any type of experience you can have outside of your home country will benefit you in your career and perspective of life. If you can get somewhere...go for it. You are young and you don't have many of the responsibilities yet that could tie you down to your local geographical area, like a job or family. Take advantage of this while you can!

I understand that some of you may have difficulty (financially or otherwise) getting out of your country. If that's the case, find ways to learn about other cultures (watch the National Geographic Channel). But nothing beats actually going there and walking on foreign soil and being immersed in another culture.

11. Keep growing.

It may seem obvious to you that you would be growing since you're in college. But I meet a lot of college students who gain knowledge, but don't gain growth. I guess I'm talking about maturity. There are many experiences that you'll have in college that can help you to grow up if you'll let them.

Current research says that adolescence is being pushed farther out - to the mid 20's. They are calling it delayed adulthood. Many young adults are simply pushing back some of the major decisions: marriage, career, home purchasing, etc - to later in life. But being young doesn't mean you have to be immature.

There are many ways to grow outside of the classroom. Life has a way of providing it's own type of classroom. Each of us has an opportunity to grow emotionally, relationally, spiritually, psychologically, and physically at different points of our lives. Take the experiences you have in life and spend time reflecting on how you can use those to become a better person. Growth isn't an automatic process. It takes work and it takes time. Use these exciting years in college to develop yourself.

It's exciting to watch Seniors walk across the stage at graduation and remember what they were like when they came in as Freshman. There is so much potential that is wrapped into each one. I love being apart of the process of unlocking that potential during their time in school. That's why I've written this book. If there's something here that you find helpful, then I've succeeded. As with any list, there's so much more that could be added.

CHAPTER SEVEN
EXCELLENT STUDENT

The word excellent is used to indicate an extremely good item or person or condition. Human beings have innate desire towards excellence in everything. For example, we desire outstanding social status, perfect physical health, exceptional life achievements, superb services, and first-rate amenities of life. The human desire for excellent things or conditions remains energetic until one's demise. At practical level, human efforts towards excellence may adopt lopsided approach, so that a person may concentrate on appearance of something ignoring its reality. For instance, a student may target only grades during learning process, while the genuine approach of learning is to focus on knowledge, wisdom, and character. Generally, people pursue admirable belongings or status rather than reasonable possessions or positions. An excellent outcome is dominantly team phenomenon, so that an excellent human achievement inevitably demands a strategically designed ambition-struggle framework, both personal as well as shared. Moreover, the nature of human ambitions and method of human struggle towards something distinguishes between mediocre and wise. A mediocre accumulates marvelous stuff of worldly items, while a wise adds excellence in physical health or enhances excellence in intellectual might or promotes excellence in moral beauty and character.

Excellent Student

Curiosity is basic human instinct. Curiosity is defined as, "A strong desire to know about something." A curious tendency of self instils a relentless desire for knowing something hidden or concealed. Conceptually, a systematic curious attitude towards knowledge enhancement shapes students. Literally, a student is a person who is studying at a school, college, etc. while studying is an activity of learning or gaining knowledge. An educator satisfies inquisitiveness of students. A student is knowledge-seeker, while an educator is knowledge-giver. A purposefully designed interactive setup of knowledge-seekers and knowledge-givers shapes educational institutions. It is noteworthy that a learning environment is designed to shape excellent students. An excellent student is the ultimate goal of multiple knowledge management activities, both academic and non-academic. An excellent student is curious basically, but creative ultimately. A curious student wants to know something unknown, now and then, while, a creative wants to make something anew, now and again. Curiosity unearths ultimate truths, while creativity makes new truths. Curiosity develops bonds with past; while creativity shapes better future. Curious is an efficient researcher, while a creative is an effective entrepreneur. Curious is a philosopher, while creative is a scientist. Curiosity lays foundation of something, while creativity erects structure. Curiosity is asking questions, while creativity is giving answers. Curiosity is to think within box, while creativity is to think outside the box. Human civilisation is synergistic totalling of curiosity and creativity. Find your perfect mix between curious and creativity to be the best student you can be.

Essential Skills of Excellent Student

Formal Learning is basically preparation or prelude of practical life. At practical level, a person needs some professional skills for reasonable earning, a few social skills for fruitful interactions, and handful personal skills for contented lifestyle. An excellent student has an evident understanding about needed professional skills. Moreover, she/he has constant desire for professional acumen. Secondly, life is an interactive phenomenon. People interact during countless occasions of life. An interaction is either productive or non-productive. It is social intelligence or social skills that prepare for productive interactions. A productive interaction is win-win and stable. An excellent student has relevant toolkit for meaningful interactive life, moreover, she/he has firm desire for social interactions. Thirdly, a sizeable portion of day is spent on personal activities such as sleeping, chatting, and exercising. The leisure time relaxes and prepares for next round of professional or interactive life. It is noteworthy that proper application of personal skills avoids boredom, fatigue, lethargy, and regrets from personal life. The prominent personal skills are: subjective thinking, lateral thinking, collective brainstorming, driving vehicles, setting social links, repairing things, gardening, increasing physical strength & stamina, writing creatively, expressing feelings through art work, capturing memorable moments through photography, etc. A stable combination of personal, social, and economic skills is inevitable repertoire of an excellent student.

Learning Methodology of an Excellent Student

Students enhance their knowledge level through absorbing lectures/syllabi. Learning through lecture is easiest way of gaining knowledge. An excellent student reads the learning matter before lecture, pays full attention on subject matter during presentation, participates in learning activity through relevant/thought-provoking questions, she/he makes notes of important points during knowledge transfer, after lecture, she/he reviews noted points and prepares personal notes and meets with the professor to cover any difficult topics before too much information is piled on top of it. A learning approach based on Preparation, Attention, Participation, Notes-Construction and Revision is an effective learning strategy.

Reviewing is vital aspect of study. Human mind remembers information through revision, both verbal as well as written, so that revision of studied matter is either verbal or written. Human mind utilises multiple techniques of revision such as loud revision, bird eye view or cursory revision, concise writing, listing of matter, teaching others, and thorough notes-making. Generally, a verbal revision is comparatively easy but less effective or quickly vanishing from memory, on the other hand written revision is relatively cumbersome but more effective and lasting. It is noteworthy that the most effective way of revision is teaching of fellow students.

Effective Goal Setting & Excellent Student

Life is goal driven phenomenon. A purposeless life is no life at all. A student can make academic goals for knowledge and non-academic goals for character. It is the responsibility of the older generation to guide students on goal setting. The academic goals are generally short run while the life goals are normally permanent or will take place within the next decade or so. A compatibility of academic goals with life goals enhances interest level of students. For example, the academic goal is to get distinction while the life goal is to shape balanced lifestyle. A distinction can be achieved through wild study schedule. The extremist approach is a negation of balanced lifestyle. A right approach for some special reward is to adopt persistent study habit with balance lifestyle. Overtime, a discrepancy may develop among multiple goals, so that, a recurrent reconsideration of academic and non-academic goals and its compatibility with life goals and future challenges is vital for consistent and sustainable growth of personality and effective for right selection of career.

Concluding Remarks - A Few Words on Bright Future

Students are generally dependents on elders (i.e., parents, teachers, etc.) during educational life. After completing education, students start practical life. A fruitful, productive, and independent practical life indicates bright future. Bright future becomes reality through compatibility of inner ambitions with outer realties. It is noteworthy that a plethora of wishful desires is unable to shape better future. A realistic, positive, and proactive attitude towards challenges/opportunities means bright future. An excellent student is knowledgeable, well-mannered and wise. The outer world or collective life follows some unchangeable maxims of life. A knowledgeable/mannered/wise person is readily prepared for and quickly adjustable on upcoming realities of outer world.

CHAPTER EIGHT
COLLEGE ROOMMATE

Whether you are moving into the dorm as a freshman, or a senior looking for a beautiful house close to campus, you definitely will be living with roommates. There are very few college students who live by themselves, mostly because it is too expensive. In university towns, rent for a single apartment can reach a high price per month. The solution to lower rent is living with roommates. In this chapter I will talk about the pros and cons of living with roommates, how to find roommates, and I'll share some experiences along the way.

Since Sandra just graduated from college, She considered herself somewhat of an expert in the college living life. Not much has changed in the few months she has been on her own. She is living by herself for the first time in her life, and let me tell you, it is quite different than attending a college.

TIPS FOR #COLLEGELIFE

Most students start off their college (campus) experience living in the dorms. When Sandra moved in, she elected to live in an old fashion dorm. Twenty some odd rooms on the floor with one large communal bathroom. The guys section was separated from the girls section by a lounge/kitchen with one stove, one oven, a few couches, and a TV. Not quite the same as living at home with her own bedroom and bathroom. Most dorms (at least the old fashion ones) do not have single rooms. Everyone has at least one roommate. Most schools give you the option to choose your roommate or have one randomly assigned to you. Sandra's freshman year, She chose to live with a friend. Make sure you are good friends with this person or else you may end up hating each other. I have had so many friends that would eventually hate their roommates. They were friends on the outside, but in the room it was hell.

Sandra was lucky for the first semester of college. She got along with her roommate for the most part. They led different lives, which was a good thing. Sandra was on the meal plan, and her roommate wasn't. They took different classes at different times and hung out with different people too. In my opinion this is how it has to be if you choose to live with a friend. (Please note that the dorms I am

TIPS FOR #COLLEGELIFE

talking about are roughly 12 x 12 with two twin beds and two desks and enough room to stand up. The new age dorms where people have their own rooms and bathrooms are totally different.) Sandra's friend whom she roomed with was transferred to a new school after their first semester for various reasons. Sandra thought she had it made in the shade. Would the school not know? Would she get the room to herself? The answer was no.

Enters Helen (her new roommate from Germany). She was an American but grew up in Germany on a military base. This is one of the best and worst experiences of university. Living with a complete stranger who is the complete opposite of you. This is every incoming freshman's worst nightmare. Helen moved in with Sandra because he was voted out of a triple dorm room by her previous roommates. Wow! After living with her for a semester, Sandra knew why they voted her out.

Sandra had nothing against being a proud citizen and wanting to serve in the military, The part when you have to wake up at 4:00 AM every morning to exercise, that's when Sandra started to lose it. Helen's alarm would go off at 3:45 A.M everyday and she would regularly hit snooze for about 30 minutes. She never went to class, so she was there to bug Sandra on all her time off. She played a lot of Call of duty.

She played it all through the night with the volume so loud you would think their dorm room was a war zone. Sandra tried to take Helen out with her, or eat lunch with her at the cafeteria, but she just couldn't take it. She learned a lot from Helen and will never forget her. Sandra's most memorable moment was when she turned the volume all the way up on her PC and blasted the Salute Your Shorts theme song right in her ear while Helen was sleeping. Sandra captured it all on video. Helen flicked her off and went to bed. She has not seen Helen since she moved out of the dorm.

Some Pros and Cons of living in the dorms (once again, I am talking about the old fashioned dorms, not the apartment style ones).

Pro - Right on campus. You can wake up five minutes before class and walk there in your dressing gown.

Pro - Right on campus. Food is close by (especially if you are on a meal plan).

Pro - Social life. You meet a lot of new people living in the dorms. Some become friends for life.

Dorms often have mini-activities and social events where everyone hangs out.

Pro - It's new. College is about experiencing new things. Dorm life is one of them.

Pro - It's cheap. Not nearly as expensive as renting an apartment.

Con - No privacy. People will just randomly walk in your room. Keep it locked.

Con - Old and dirty dorms are no fun.

Con - Dorms are very small. You won't be able to fit everything you have in your closet.

Con - Having annoying roommates that you can do nothing about.

Con - Internet firewalls. Some dorms are really strict now about what you can and cannot do on the school's internet.

Con – Sharing a kitchen and bathroom. Everyone has different standards of hygiene.

Con – Fire alarm test at random times in the day or night.

CHAPTER NINE
THREE KINGS

This chapter is a very important part of this book which must not be overlooked. Let's look at three essential personalities as reference for proper comprehension and understanding of this book.

King Saul

King saul was a great king, his reign as king was very important and noteable to all that were under is governance, the reason I am referencing to King Saul is because he made a lot of errors and mistakes that proved to be disastrous, and I would like to share his experience with students in higher Institution. Here are some things to look at;

1. King Saul's bad sacrifices

"So Saul said, 'Bring burnt offering and peace offerings here to me.' And he offered the burnt offering."- 1 Samuel 13:9

He made a very bad sacrifice as a king, and while he was ruling, because of his great position, forgetting it wasn't his duty to do so. Students should make sacrifices that are good and important to their life and education, bad sacrifices such as absconding class for a late-out or leaving your assignment undone for a sporting event, will choke you up.

2. King Saul didn't keep the commandments

"And Samuel said to Saul, 'You have done foolishly, you have not kept the commandment of the Lord your God, which He commanded you. For now, the Lord would have established your kingdom over Israel forever."- 1 Samuel 13:13

As a student you should be law abiding both on and off campus, You should have an out a plan or time table or even a day to day schedule as the case may be for your personal upbringing.

3. King Saul was disobedient

All student must be obedient to all their professors, and they must not despise guidance and counselling from their lecturers at the higher institution.

In 1 Sam 15:3 God commanded Saul to fight and totally destroy Amalek for their attack against Israel. Rather than do God's command, Saul killed all the people of Amalek and undesirable livestock but spared Agag, the king, and the goodly sheep of Amalek. Samuel who was not only displeased but also insisted on complete obedience, scolded Saul and rejected Saul's excuses.

Saul's motive may have appeared good in his mind, but Samuel knew the mind of God and insisted until the counsel of God was executed. Saul's self-will made him lose his kingship. He did not repent at the correction by Samuel. King David was different, though. When Nathan confronted David over what he did, he admitted it, he wrote a Psalm to let Israel know what he had done wrong. He did not pretend; he accepted the rebuke and correction of God's servant, and God said he was a man after his own heart. The sin David committed was more terrible than that of Saul, but the issue is not about what we do wrong, but when we are confronted with the deed, whether we accept the wrong, then repent, confessing our sins, or whether we defend our actions.

4. King Saul was distracted

It is just a mere talk if we say we can't be distracted, Since we live in a world full of influences which has a high rate amongst university students. Distractions will come but you should focus more on your character, goals and purpose.

5. King Saul was jealous of King David

"Then Saul was very angry, and the saying displeased him; and he said, 'They have ascribed to David ten thousands, and to me they have ascribed only thousands. Now, what more can he have but the kingdom?' So Saul eyed David from that day forward."- 1 Samuel 18:8-9

King Saul was jealous of David's achievement and victory over Goliath.

Don't be jealous of another person's achievement in academics or in life because his success came as a result of dedication and commitment, just continue with what you do and work harder towards being successful and you will get there.

King Solomon

Solomon was a great and popular king, he was known for his wisdom and understanding, which he used to rule over his people and to possess a lot of wealth. Let's check out some great mistakes he made even though he was known as a wise king.

1. King Solomon's great wealth

"King Solomon was richer and wiser than any other king in the world."- 2 Chronicles 9:22

Solomon's great wealth made him turned away from God. No matter your level of intelligence or academic achievement in the higher institution, it is still important to be humble. Don't be non-challant to everyone on your level and the ones superior to you, even in your studies. Be humble so you can be recognised after your time at the college.

2. King Solomon disobeyed God

As you can clearly see this issue of disobedience causes a lot of disaster even to great men in life, so be obedient and learn from the wisdom of others.

3. Kings Solomon's promiscuity

"King Solomon, however, loved many foreign women besides Pharaoh's daughter- Moabites, Ammonites, Edomites, Sidonians and Hittites. They were from nations about which the Lord had told the Israelites, 'You must not intermarry with them, because they will surely turn your hearts after their gods.' Nevertheless, Solomon held fast to them in love. He had seven hundred wives of royal birth and three hundred concubines, and his wives led him astray."-1 Kings 11:1-3

Everyone knows about the great record which Solomon laid down; he had 700 wives and 300 concubines. Sometimes I do not know how he was able to talk to one thousand women about love, and they all concurred to him, but I remembered that he was also anointed but he misused his anointing.

Don't be distracted by the opposite sex, advances from the opposite sex will hinder your potential for success at the university. You already know that there is a great attraction between opposite sexes that is natural after 12 and 13 years old, this is so that you are disciplined in this before you get married, so you must master it not kill it. When you deny it, you become stronger, but if you give in to every desire of yours, you become a slave of that desire. If you are too close with someone of the opposite sex, it is like holding two polarised magnets together. How far can you hold two magnets together without it touching? It will always touch when you bring them close, if they are far away you can keep them apart but the closer you bring them together the attraction is very strong, with magnet it touches quickly without you hunting it, this is what happens when a boy and a girl come close even when they determine not to contact each other.

King David

King david is a mighty personality in the bible that every young individual should learn from. He was young but he made a great impact in Israel. Let's go straight to the things we ought to learn from David.

1. King David was dedicated

Dedicate your life to your dreams, don't lose sight of your goals and aspirations.

2. King David's boldness

"And David said to Saul, 'Let no man's heart fail because of him; your servant will go and fight with this Philistine.'"- 1 Samuel 17:32

He had the boldness of a lion (His boldness was because His God was with him) though he was young and small in stature. As a student in the college be ready to face every challenge you encounter in your education, don't see it as a wall, see it as a stepping stone to your success.

3. King David's courage

Always believe in God and his word, he will help you have the courage and the will to be successful, keep in mind that you will succeed through His help.

4. Kings David's consistency

King David's consistency made him famous and known all over Israel, be consistent in what you do, be consistent in reading, studying, and carrying out research. By so doing you are feeding your focus and you are starving your distractions.

Things to learn from the three kings;

King Saul and King Solomon had a lot of things that came easy to them. They possessed so much but ultimately lost humility and drive.

When they were in training, they had an easy life; they did not go through suffering which could have exercised their skills in preparation for when they will reign as king, or in your case when you will be doctors, programmers, scientist or lawyers. King David was planning for his future at a very tender age, he went through many battles, suffered so much which made him proficient in all the skills that he needed to reign as king. Don't dodge little challenges that will sharpen you, seek to solve the small problems now, because it will help you with more significant problems later in life.

Earlier on Saul and Solomon had lived a comfortable life, so their reign as king was disastrous, but King David's reign was such a successful one because he did not have an easy life, at College per say, he exercised himself and won, he was not tired or weary racing with footmen, so when he has to compete with horses, he was able to.

Jeremiah 12:5"If racing against mere men makes you tired, how will you race against horses?

If you stumble and fall on open ground, what will you do in the thickets near the Jordan?

So students, should you be like David, you will live to witness your successful reign as a lawyer, doctor, engineer, or whatever your future ambition may be.

CHAPTER TEN
OUTSTANDING STUDENT

While many students lack study skills and need to develop more, my experience as a lecturer, tutor, and long-time student is that study skills aren't the biggest need. Most students have the necessary skills to study effectively. Most possess useful knowledge of note taking strategies, memorisation techniques, planning, organisation, and reading strategies.

The bigger need is not expand their study skills, but rather to refine and specialise in the skills they already have.

For students who are interested in achieving academic success, knowing these five elements will become a simple yet comprehensive tool that can help them approach every academic assignment with confidence.

1. Know your educational opportunity.

For most students education is the most important opportunity of their lifetime. The degree to which secondary school and college students understand this will affect the outcome of their education.

It's essential to note, that being more motivated doesn't necessarily ensure students will remember more or do better on a test.

However, it has everything to do with focus, clarity, drive, and stick-to-it attitude. Without a clear goal in mind for ultimate success, students will struggle during those long, gruelling Physics sessions, organic chemistry, or mathematics. Few people enjoy those subjects. There must be something other than "fun" that keeps a student going.

If you know your educational opportunity, you can find that motivation.

2. Know how an idea works.

Education is all about ideas. Some students miss this fundamental point. There is a tendency to enjoy either the overarching ideas, what I call the "Big Ideas" - or the specific facts, the details that explain that Big Idea.

Some students are fantastic at explaining the major themes, movements, or events that move a class along; however, they can tend to miss the small important details that make all the difference. People, places, events, dates, and anything that requires flash cards, tend to get overlooked.

On the other hand, some students make thousands of flash cards, memorise hundreds of dates, can give the middle name of every president, but cannot put them together in a coherent way to make a point in an essay. Knowing these two complementary elements of ideas is a vital task for every student.

Successful students understand how ideas work, can follow the movement of those ideas, and explain it in an exam.

3. Know what makes an effective study session.

Success or failure is largely determined on study sessions. Great study sessions leave students feeling sure of themselves. Their brains hurt. They're tired. But the responsible adult inside all of them feels great.

Study periods will make or break a student. Successful students invest the energy into learning how to solve their problems.

4. Know how to live the lifestyle of a successful student.

No one can compartmentalise his or her life. The lie that your exercise habits, sleep schedule, and chosen recreation have no effect on your mind, emotions, or will is unwise. Most people believe it, but it is still not true. Every student has one life. Family, friends, athletics, volunteerism, and academics are all parts of the same life that cannot ever truly be separated. Each area influences the others.

If you've ever had to take an exam with the flu or after a major break-up with a long-time significant friend, you've experienced the way one event can effect another in your life. Your physical condition influences your emotional condition, which influences your mental condition and influences your relational condition. It's a cycle that successful students leverage to their advantage, and unsuccessful students ignore.

Depression, for example, could have many causes. Sometimes chemical imbalances cause depression. Sometimes a lack of sleep causes it. If that's you, you could be depressed. If you experience a depressing life event, seek help.

Similarly, academic success requires a lifestyle that breeds health in every area. Diet, exercise, rest, relaxation, and stress relief all play a part in the development of successful students.

5. Know how to complete the required tasks.

Some things in life just require the right know how. I don't know how to fly a plane, scuba dive, change my truck's transmission, or build a salt-water aquarium. Accordingly, I don't do those things.

But students assigned a twenty page research paper or a book report are not at liberty to decline a project. They have to perform these tasks, so they must know how.

Additionally, some tasks are hard just because students haven't learned the proper technique to finishing them successfully. The good news is that there are resources available for teaching students effective ways to accomplish every task they will encounter at school. The important key is whether or not those students will invest the energy needed to learn those skills.

CHAPTER ELEVEN
HOW TO BE SAFE ON CAMPUS

University brings more freedom and fewer restrictions than most students have experienced during their secondary school years. Newly minted undergraduates have a positive view of their fellow students and take for granted that they and their possessions are safe. Many college students are unaware of the consequences that might arise from certain social situations.

General Campus Safety

Students can do the most to reduce their risk of becoming a victim of theft or assault by remembering to lock their doors when they leave (even just to do their laundry), keeping valuables (laptops, ipods, etc) out of plain site, closing windows on the first floor and ensuring that anytime they access a secure building that they are aware of other individuals entering the building under their access card swipe.

TIPS FOR #COLLEGELIFE

Most college campuses are walker friendly if a few precautions are kept in mind:

- Be aware of your surroundings and surrounding people.

- Embrace the buddy system. Try and find a friend you can go to new place with.

- Walk in well-lit areas.

- Don't look like a victim - walk confidently, directly and at a steady pace.

- Walk close to the curb, avoid alleys, bushes and doorways.

- Don't be afraid to make a scene - if you are in danger scream, run or yell (to draw attention to your situation).

Many campuses set up text alert programs for their student population realising this is the most effective way to communicate potential safety hazards to students in a timely manner. If a security concern is happening on campus the text messages keep students informed on what to do until they receive an all-clear message. Check with your campus police or office of student safety to register for this important alert system.

CHAPTER TWELVE
MONEY MANAGEMENT
FOR STUDENTS

The college years can be the best of times and the worst of times. It's great to finally be on your own, making new friends, getting the education to embark in a career; and to socialise freely without the supervision of your parents. It can be the worst of times as you see your bank account getting smaller, having to manage your student loan/financial aid funds, your personal funds and your school work all at the same time.

So, how can you manage your money better as a college student?

ONE: Whenever you notice you have more month than money it's always best to track your spending. Where is my money going? The easiest and cheapest way is to take a notebook out and start listing everything you're spending money on; and I mean everything. From every day necessities to small splurges that can often go unnoticed such as coffee, snacks and drinks. If you have a bank account go ahead and pull past bank statements and see what you've been spending on outside of basic necessities; eating out? Cable? Internet? Expensive cell phone package?

TWO: Create a budget. Just as you have an outline of what you must do to graduate in your degree of choice, you also need an outline of how to manage the money that is coming in on a monthly basis. It should include the total amount of money coming in from all sources - scholarship, part time job, parents, etc; as well as an 'outline' on what you should be spending it on. Necessities come first of course; followed by 'extras'. The #1 rule of budgeting is to ensure you always have more income than expenses. So, if you notice those 'extras' that you've listed in Step #1, are cutting into your income; you have 2 options:

THREE: Start cutting. This is the perfect time in your life to learn how to separate 'wants' from 'needs'. No matter what stage you are in life, there will always be something you cannot afford; it's best to learn that lesson now. This is not to say you cannot have fun; by all means enjoy your University years! But, do so by eliminating unnecessary expenses that hinder you from truly making this time of your life enjoyable; namely from being broke J. The key is to save and then splurge. Cutting expenses doesn't always have to involve eliminating; for example:

Prior to buying books for the class, wait until you get the syllabus to see if you really need the book.

Find someone that has just taken the class and do a book exchange.

If you're purchasing your books; rent them instead.

Evaluate your meal plan; does it fit your needs or did you get a bigger plan than what you are actually consuming - meaning you're wasting money each month.

Use that Student ID! There are discounts for students everywhere you go - the movies, the bus, car insurance, health insurance, restaurants, airfare, train, etc - you name it; make sure you ask before you spend. Identify the places that will allow you to get more bang for your

University buck. If they don't discount; patronise a business that does.

Leave your car at home. Campus life is all about walk ability; and public transportation is pretty rampant. Why add on car insurance, gas and maintenance to an already strained budget; you'll be able to get around just fine.

Take advantage of free University events. Uuniversities are known to hold a variety of free social events, some even come with free food!

FOUR: Earn more money. This is an option if your schedule permits. I'd think carefully about this one, as your ability to meet your educational requirements is way more important than 'living large'. If it's necessary to take on a part time job just to meet basic needs, then please make sure it's one that will accommodate your school schedule. A campus position is a good place to start. And if you do find a position off campus, see if they offer tuition assistance as one of their benefits; every little bit helps!

FIVE: Develop Your Mindset. This means that once you know what you make, how much your expenses are, you've cut some of your 'extras' and/or have taken on a part time job; your mindset should switch from spending ALL of your money left over after expenses, to starting

TIPS FOR #COLLEGELIFE

to establish a savings, making sure all of your bills are paid on time. If you don't have a bank account, this is the perfect time to open one and actually learn how to balance your account. Establishing a money mindset is all about being aware of your InCOME in comparison to your OutGO, and making the necessary changes to retain as much of your InCOME as possible.

SIX: Discuss your financial aid with your F.A. officer so that you're aware of any scholarships or grants you may be eligible for. Find out what type of aid you are receiving - free or those that have to be paid back - and what requirements are needed to keep receiving those free aid funds; find out what interest rates are tied to the loan portion of your financial aid..

SEVEN: Monitor for continued success! Very rarely do our income and expenses remain the same month after month; year after year, especially on a University budget. Monitor your budget often, especially when unexpected money is received or unexpected expenses arise to make sure your pounds/dollars are working in your behalf.

TIPS FOR #COLLEGELIFE

Some Personal Safety and Self Defense Tips

The incidence of criminal assault on most University campuses has steadily increased year after year. What do you do to secure your safety when it comes time for you to leave for University? "Good question?" you might ask. Well, you would not be the first to have serious reservations about going out into the unpredictable world of University life.

Crime is on the rise and there are few places more inviting to criminals than a campus full of students who are unprepared for life on their own. Not enough kids these days are taught the important lessons of personal safety and self defence. Although campus security has greatly improved over the past few years on many College campuses, the main impetus for staying safe lies primarily with each and every University student. Knowledge is power, and knowledge of how to protect yourself can be life saving.

While personal safety and self defence may seem like the same thing, they really are quite different. Personal safety is all about modifying your actions and behavior in a manner that will preclude ones self from being a prime target of crime. Self defense is about knowing how to protect one's self when they are being attacked.

Below, I would like to offer some tips which should greatly reduce the risk of you from becoming another entry on the list of crime statistics.

Tips for Being Safe on (or off) Campus:

Whether you are living on campus in a dormitory, a house, or some off campus apartment, the first order of business should be to secure your home. You can accomplish this by making sure all doors and windows are closed and locked when away. Even while at home, it is a good idea to keep doors and windows locked. However, this is sometimes not easy to do. There are a wide variety of alarms and security devices suitable for protecting your living quarters from intruders. They are very effective and can be used both while you are home as well as away. These include motion detectors, door stop alarms, wireless intruder alarms, and more.

You should become familiar with your neighbors and be aware of who should be hanging around your dormitory or apartment and who should not. Keep an eye out for strangers hanging out around your home. Often times students are followed home and "spied" on for a period of time in order to learn their routines. For added security, consider security cameras to keep an eye on entryways.

When you return home, whether in daylight or after dark, remember these tips. Don't hang around on the porch or entryway. Most attackers usually strike as you enter the home. Upon entering, if something looks out-of-place, don't continue. Exit the building and go for help. Never re-enter the house until someone can verify that it is safe.

If you have a car, check around the car and inside the car before entering. When entering your car, open the door, enter quickly, and lock the doors. Most times, attackers make their move when the victim is about to enter their vehicle.

Always walk with a friend, or better yet, in a group. Carry some form of personal safety device such as a personal alarm. These devices are inexpensive and offer a great deal of defense towards an attacker.

If you carry a purse or wallet, keep them close to your body or hidden in an inside pocket. Do not carry large sums of money with you. It is a good idea to have a second wallet or purse containing only enough money for the evening and nothing else. Do this when you know you

TIPS FOR #COLLEGELIFE

will not need a driver's license or other forms of personal identification.

Always travel in well populated areas. Don't take the dark, untraveled short-cut, especially at night. Be sure your path is well lighted and away from areas where an attacker could hide. Avoid isolated areas. Walk on the side of the street facing the traffic. If approached by someone riding in a car, run in the opposite direction the vehicle is traveling. Try to stay near the curb when walking on the sidewalk, keeping your distance from dark building entryways. Be cautious of anyone approaching asking for directions, passing out flyers, or asking for the time. Do not loan your mobile/cell phone to anyone. If you wish to offer assistance, offer to make the call for them.

If you feel uneasy, like someone is following you, go immediately to the nearest busy location such as a place of business or a busy public area. If you are carrying a personal alarm, have it out and ready for use. If you encounter a dangerous situation, cry out for help by yelling "help". Many times a cry for "help" is ignored because people don't want to get involved, or fear for their own safety. Yelling "help" usually attracts attention even from those who are just curious.

Learn to defend yourself. Nothing will deter an attacker more than someone's ability to defend them self. Most attackers are looking for a "willing" victim. You can imagine their surprise when their victim begins to yell loudly, punch or kick, or use a personal protection device. Women especially have to learn not to be afraid of their attacker; rather, they should respect their own right to protect themselves and offer any resistance necessary to drive them away.

Become informed. As I mentioned earlier, knowledge is power. Learn the art of self defense. Investigate the many personal safety products available which are specifically designed with your protection in mind. They may someday save your life.

Would you love some Time Management Tips also?

In the midst of football games, hanging out with friends and finding a source for your next meal, where do you find time for writing papers, studying for exams, reading, and going to the gym? Have you ever fallen into the trap of just not having enough time for everything you need to get done? You may have noticed that this is one of the most common challenges that people face, and yet there are volumes of books written on this topic. Still, the problem persists and is prevalent in almost everyone's life at one time or another.

The following tips are written with your best intentions in mind . . . having as much fun as humanly possible, while also meeting the requirements placed on you by schools, parents, and professors. There is a way to get it all done; you just have to be smart about it and have a plan. So, here is where you begin:

1. Acknowledge Your Priorities. This one is tricky. Notice I said to acknowledge your priorities. This means, take a good look at your life and acknowledge (be aware of) the priorities that you typically assign to the various areas in your life. If you can acknowledge that you consistently give a particular area of your life the highest priority, you might find that this either needs to be changed or you need to find a way to make this priority work within your life (meeting your other obligations as well). It's okay if your main priority right now is hanging out with your friends . . . as long as this priority does not prevent you from meeting your other priorities and obligations as a student. Understand that the fact that you are in University means that the obligations associated

with that (studying, reading, writing papers) automatically become a priority. Of course, this may not be by choice but your success in this area of life is dependent upon your making it a priority. Conflicting priorities can be a challenge but once you acknowledge that you have several equal priorities, you will be able to better schedule your time and energy to encompass them all.

2. Plan Ahead. Your professors give you a syllabus for a reason. Knowing what's due throughout the semester can help you plan out how you can finish the assignment, while also maintaining your social life and activities. For example, let's say you have an essay due in two weeks. During this same two weeks there are two football games, two get-togethers, two exams, and all of your regular classes to attend. If you want to do it all and maintain your GPA, schedule in time to study for your exams and write your essay during timeframes that you can commit to keeping. Make yourself follow through on your plan and you will be having your fun with no conscience about remaining homework that hasn't been finished or studying that hasn't been done. Remember tip #1? Keep your priorities in mind when you plan. Your priorities are the

absolute first things that should be scheduled into your plan. If you do this, everything else will fall into place so much easier because you've already accomplished the most important things that needed to be done.

3. Multi-Task . . . Selectively. Studying for a test is not the ideal time to multi-task! Many students study on the couch in front of the television or at their computer with email and Facebook open. Memory retention reduces significantly when you're not focused 100% on what you're doing. Rather than getting two things done at once, this actually works as a deficit and ends up wasting more time than you've spent. Conversely, going to the gym may be a great time to get some cardio and reading done at the same time. Use your time wisely. If you know you have a fifteen minute walk across campus at 10:30am, plan to do something productive during that walking time, such as making necessary phone calls or eating a snack between classes. Similarly, if you have a fifteen minute break between classes across the hall from each other, you can utilise that time to go over your notes or briefly read a chapter. That fifteen minutes of studying can give you some extra time with your friends later!

4. Know Your Limits. We live in an instant gratification and "do-it-all" environment, which is sometimes unrealistic in terms of the endless opportunities that are presented to us every day. Your priorities are number one and should be treated accordingly. However, if you find that giving attention to your priorities leaves you with no time for anything else, you may be doing too much. At this point it would be necessary to re-evaluate your priorities to see if there is anything there that can be adjusted so that you have an opportunity for "down time" every once in awhile. An endless schedule of constant rush, worry, and anxiety usually results in very high stress levels, which in turn may cause a number of other health issues. Weight gain, migraine headaches, depression and hair loss are just a few effects that chronic stress can have on your health. Take care of yourself and remember that you have control over your own priorities and your schedule.

5. Be Responsible. As stated earlier, some of your priorities may not be those that you would choose if you didn't have to. Remember that this is only one stage in your life and the choices you make now truly do have an affect on your success in life down the road. If studying is not your

favorite pastime (and whose is?), just remember that it's a stepping stone to where you want to go. Graduation day will come and go and then you'll be free from the books and on to your new career. Being responsible with your time is a choice . . . one that you will be thankful for when you land your dream job!

Using these time management tips will give you a strategy to live productively, manage your life effectively, and have more free time in your schedule for the things you love to do.

CHAPTER THIRTEEN
COLLEGE HEALTH RISK

University life can be the best of times and the worst of times. For most young people going off to college is a time of excitement. They envision living with some autonomy from their parents and anticipate meeting new people and experiencing new things. However, sometimes experience turns into too much experimentation and autonomy develops into homesickness and depression.

Campus life is a huge transition for young people and has its own set of health risks. Below are the top 5 health risks for college students:

1. Sleep deprivation: Studies find that up to 20% of college students suffer from sleeping disorders. It is common for college students to experience altered sleeping patterns

TIPS FOR #COLLEGELIFE

when they leave home for the dorms. Their new sleeping environment is complicated by unusual schedules, which fluctuate due to class schedules, social activities and work. Many students stay up late to cram for exams or social excessively. Sleep deprivation leads to increased irritability, anxiety and even weight gain.

Solution: The average adult should get between 6-8 hours of sleep per night. Experts suggest that exercise can help establish healthy sleeping patterns. It is recommended that students exercise at least three hours before bedtime, never just before bedtime. If you cannot get a full night's sleep on a regular basis the next best thing is to schedule "catch-up" nights a few days a week. Students should make a concentrated effort to get a block of sleep on these "catch-up" nights. This practice will help prevent long-term health issues.

2. Eating disorders: Gaining the extra freshman pounds is bad enough, but it won't kill you. Anorexia nervosa and Bulimia nervosa are a different matter. Both conditions arise out of a need for control and acceptance. When the pressures of college life are too great some young womem (less of a problem for male students) focus on calories and their weight in an effort to block out other problems. Eating disorders may be used as a way to express control when the rest of life seems out of control. Girls suffering from bulimia will eat to avoid feeling overwhelmed, lonely, sad, or depressed. When they purge, whether by vomiting or compulsively exercising, it helps them feel like they are releasing all those feelings and again gaining a sense of control.

Solution: Eating disorders are severe problems that will require professional help. Most universities have a health center, which can get a student connected to the appropriate health professionals. If you suspect your roommate or friend to be struggling with this issue talk with them and be supportive and encourage them to seek professional help, eating disorders have complex psychological backgrounds probably beyond your ability to correct, so supporting them to seek professional help might save your friends life.

CHAPTER FOURTEEN
STUDENTS CAMPUS FELLOWSHIP

Anthony and Antonia are 18-year-old set of twins, they both were lovely teens who gained admission to the same college. The college lifestyle for each of them changed them, and that revealed to the parents who they really were. Anthony went out and saw all the lovely things he had longed for, but could not have because he was under the care of his parents, but now that he had all the time in the world to explore these, he went for them. He went out of his upbringing standard because his heart had always been on other things he could not have at home. College life only gave him an opportunity to show who he really was. Antonia, on the other hand, made deliberate effort to search for a campus fellowship, where she joined a couple of students to study the bible for an hour every Thursday evening at 7 pm, and she quickly integrated herself into the system because of the new friends she made. She had students who are years ahead of her on the course and got much help from them which helped her to settle down much faster than other students. This act alone of joining the fellowship, shielded her from most things that happened on the campus and made her strong and grow spiritually, socially and academically.

When she went outside the territory of the home she was able to still take a stand, she found it difficult to live otherwise as it was strange to her. So, she definitely came back to the value system her parents had instilled in her as a child. Anthony was always on his new game. He was always online. To be honest, Antonia was worried about him. He wasn't always like this, she said to him, "Gaming is cool, don't get me wrong, but isn't there a point at which he could just say enough is enough?" He just kept playing and playing. There are loads of games that turn teenagers to zombies. She looked at him amazed by the way his mind worked. How could he go about devaluing his life like this? Somebody needed to set him straight.

Antonia, who really loved her brother, invited him to the group she was attending but he never turned up till one day when someone else invited him to a similar group outside campus and he went but he did not like it there because it was more of a place for older people and he liked the result his sister was getting in all her grades because of the people she was hanging around with. He saw that his sister was always happy, joyful and loved by her group, so he made an effort to do the same.

Many young people change their ways and lifestyles as soon as they get admission to a college.

So, as a freshman, with freedom at your disposal, a lot of opportunities to misuse that freedom will be opened to you. Before you get led astray, it's better you know why you're there in the first place. Anthony got a twist of fate with the wrong foot he took first, but if not for his sister, he would've lost the life which was so precious to him.

As you're entering the college, ensure that you embrace the one who knew you before you were formed in your mother's womb, and can give you expected end. Locate a student campus fellowship in your College; fellowship with them and be part of God's kingdom. As you do this, every other thing will be settled.

The student campus fellowship is another guaranteed way to meet with people: those who are not up to you spiritually and those who are more than you too. You'll establish a bond with them, and that alone can serve as a ladder of success for you where you least expect it.

Remember, all these had to do with timing. You can be involved in these and still make an excellent result. It's not about the time, but rather proper planning.

Please Leave a 1-click Review!

I would be incredibly thankful if you could take just 60 seconds to write a brief review on the platform of purchase, even if it's just a few sentences!

CONCLUSION

Well I hope this book has eased the pressure for some students who are going through ups and downs in the college. All I can say is that university is a challenge but, if you adopt any of the tips in this book, it can be quite rewarding. There is no shame in admitting to yourself that university is not as you perceived it to be like, this is the first stage of growth & I assure you, if you give it all you've got college will definitely be a better place (for current students) or the best place (for freshman). Besides, at the end of the day, the academic semesters fly by so, you might as well make the most of it.

Other Books You'll Love!

1. <u>Healthy Habits for Kids: Positive Parenting Tips for Fun Kids Exercises, Healthy Snacks and Improved Kids Nutrition</u>

2. <u>Mini Habits for Happy Kids: Proven Parenting Tips for Positive Discipline and Improving Kids' Behavior</u>

3. <u>Financial Tips to Help Kids: Proven Methods for Teaching Kids Money Management and Financial Responsibility</u>

4. <u>Life Strategies for Teenagers: Positive Parenting Tips and Understanding Teens for Better Communication and a Happy Family</u>

5. <u>101 Tips for Child Development: Proven Methods for Raising Children and Improving Kids Behavior with Whole Brain Training</u>

6. <u>101 Tips For Helping With Your Child's Learning: Proven Strategies for Accelerated Learning and Raising Smart Children Using Positive Parenting Skills</u>

7. <u>Parenting Teen Boys in Today's Challenging World: Proven Methods for Improving Teenagers Behaviour with Whole Brain Training</u>

8. Parenting Teen Girls in Today's Challenging World: Proven Methods for Improving Teenagers Behaviour with Whole Brain Training

9. The Fear of The Lord: How God's Honour Guarantees Your Peace

10. Tips for #CollegeLife: Powerful College Advice for Excelling as a College Freshman

11. The Motivated Young Adult's Guide to Career Success and Adulthood: Proven Tips for Becoming a Mature Adult, Starting a Rewarding Career, and Finding Life Balance

12. Career Success Formula Proven Career Development Advice And Finding Rewarding Employment For Young Adults And College Graduates

13. Developing Yourself as a Teenager

14. Guide for Boarding School Life

REFERENCES

- Saengpassa, Chularat. "SOTUS activities : Is it time to stop old system of seniority, tradition?". Retrieved 21 November 2014.

- Riordan, R. B., Scarf, D., & Conner, T. S. (2015), "Is orientation week a gateway to persistent alcohol use in university students? A preliminary investigation.", Journal of Studies on Alcohol and Drugs, 76: 204–2011, doi:10.15288/jsad.2015.76.204

- Greg Gottesman; Daniel Baer (2004). College Survival. Peterson's. p. 41. ISBN 0-7689-1444-2.

- Laurie Rozakis (2001). The Complete Idiot's Guide to College Survival. Alpha Books. p. 16. ISBN 0-02-864169-8.

- Studentification: A Guide to Opportunities, Challenges and Practice

- Van Ness, Norm (2012-10-23). "'Freshman' title dumped for more P.C. 'First Year Student'". Retrieved 2015-01-10.

www.ingramcontent.com/pod-product-compliance
Lightning Source LLC
Chambersburg PA
CBHW070054120526
44588CB00033B/1439